Hypnos

THE
SEAGULL
LIBRARY OF
FRENCH
LITERATURE

René Char

Hypnos

NOTES FROM THE FRENCH RESISTANCE
1943–44

TRANSLATED BY MARK HUTCHINSON

LONDON NEW YORK CALCUTTA

This work is published with the support of
Institut français en Inde – Embassy of France in India

Seagull Books, 2021

First published in French as *Feuillets d'Hypnos* by René Char
© Editions Gallimard, Paris, 1946

First published in English translation by Seagull Books, 2014
English translation © Mark Hutchinson, 2014

ISBN 978 0 8574 2 869 1

British Library Cataloguing-in-Publication Data
A catalogue record for this book is available
from the British Library

Typeset by Seagull Books, Calcutta, India
Printed and bound by Hyam Enterprises, Calcutta, India

CONTENTS

In July 1945, eleven months after the liberation of France and two months after the Act of Military Surrender in Berlin had brought the war in Europe to a close, René Char wrote to his long-time confidant and friend, the poet, Gilbert Lely, 'I had the good fortune to recover recently the journal I kept at Céreste, concealed in a hole in a wall when I left for Algiers. This is the journal I'm going to publish (a sort of Marcus Aurelius!). I'm tidying it up, abridging or expanding as the case may be. . . . It is at any rate new in my work (none of that jingoistic, resistance article stuff).'

Based on a notebook Char kept during his time in the Maquis, *Feuillets d'Hypnos* was first published in 1946 in the Gallimard Espoir series edited by Albert Camus. Unlike much of the literature inspired by the French Resistance, it was not written for propaganda purposes, nor was it motivated by any specific political or nationalist agenda. Composed of 237 'leaves' or fragments, it is a series of private notes and reflections not initially intended for publication (hence the allusion to the *Meditations* of Marcus Aurelius) and, at the same time, a carefully crafted work of literature, recollected in the relative tranquility of post-Liberation France.

As sector head for landing operations and parachute drops in the Basses-Alpes (today the Alpes-de-Haute-Provence), Char had been flown out to Algiers in July 1944 to help prepare the Allied invasion of southern France. When he returned at the end of August to Céreste, the village in the mountainous Lubéron region where he had his headquarters, he retrieved the notebook, which he had buried along with other papers in the cellar of a house, and copied out the passages corresponding to his private journal. The notebook was then destroyed, with the exception of a single 'specimen' page on which Fragments 179 and 180 of the published text are jotted down among items of book-keeping such as 'Doctor [for] Félix: frs 100' and 'Purchase [of] wheat, 3 sacks of 80 kilos: frs 3.250', and a rather ominous-sounding note to himself, 'What did that woman in the black cape want?'

Char's decision to publish the journal was prompted in part, I imagine, by a desire to capitalize on the success of his first postwar collection of poetry, *Seuls demeurent*, published in February 1945 to great acclaim, and more importantly, perhaps, by the need to bring this difficult chapter in his life to a close. Not officially relieved of his military duties until September 1945, Char had spent much of the previous year in Avignon, winding up local Resistance cells, helping his companions settle back into civilian life and organizing relief for families widowed and orphaned by the war. What we know of his life at the time suggests that he was not only oppressed by the atmosphere of denunciations and reprisals but also tormented by doubts and misgivings about the cost to himself and to others of his activities in the Maquis.

There was a political dimension as well. Post-Liberation France was awash with competing narratives about the Resistance, foremost among them the rather exaggerated claims made by the French Communist Party. It was also a period of special courts and committees and blacklists, as the Provisional Government set up under De Gaulle set about purging the country of collaborators. Like others who had played a significant role in the Resistance, Char was invited to sit on the jury of the High Court set up in November 1944 to try members of the Vichy government, but, having little faith in the formal machinery of justice, declined. He did, however, want his vision of the Resistance to play a part in the fledgling Fourth Republic and, to that end, urged his editor at Gallimard, Raymond Queneau, to get the book into print in time for the legislative elections in October 1945 that would determine the constituent assembly responsible for drafting the new constitution. For editorial reasons, this proved impossible, though he did manage to have a large excerpt published in time in the review *Fontaine*. The book went on sale seven months later, in May 1946.

Since Char destroyed the original notebook, it is impossible to say how much of the published text—which, according to his correspondence with Lely, was completed in just over three weeks—is a literal transcription of his war-time journal and how much of it was worked up in the summer of 1945. There is even some doubt as to that dating, since an early partial typescript exists which is dated 1944. We do know, on the other hand, that three of the more dramatic episodes related in the book are not an exact record of events. In Fragment 99, the presence and capture of the girl have been added (the only woman present at the time was a farm girl who had witnessed the scene from afar and alerted the villagers). Similarly, in Fragment 128, Char has introduced the episode with the young mason and has invested the villagers with something of the collective grandeur of a Greek chorus in the scene in which they surge forward over the SS; he has also moved himself from a house on the edge of the village, where he was actually hiding, to a house on the main square, at the centre of the action. And, as I explain in a separate note, neither Char nor any of his comrades was present at the execution of Roger Bernard evoked in Fragment 138.

The book, then, is in some measure a work of literary re-creation, though the liberties Char has taken in what, from a historian's perspective, might be considered the most questionable of these retellings—the execution of Roger Bernard—are justified, in my view, by the need to bring out the starkness of the decision that was forced upon him and the savagery of the Nazi reprisals. As one of his biographers has remarked, there are no 'good' Germans in *Hypnos*. For Char, the rise of Nazi Germany was not just one more chapter in the history of human tyranny but a wholly new species of evil, a catastrophe that was poisoning the wells of being.

As for the book itself, it needs only the briefest of summaries here. Written in a lapidary prose that owes as much to Heraclitus and La Rochefoucauld as it does to any of Char's contemporaries, it is quite unlike any other book written about the French Resistance—or indeed in the literature of war. There is an atmosphere both of intense solitude and of great political community, in the noblest sense of that term. Much of its pathos and moral beauty is bound up with the chaos and complexity of Occupied France; with the contrast, that is, between the magnitude of the issues confronted and the intimate, almost private, character of the response; and with the terrible burden of responsibility this placed on the movement's leaders. Its occasional obscurities I have touched on in the notes; the beauty and forcefulness of the writing are, I trust, self-evident.

Mark Hutchinson
Paris, 2014

Hypnos

1943–44

Hypnos took hold of winter and dressed it in granite. Winter turned to sleep and Hypnos to fire. The rest is man's affair.

The following notes owe nothing to self-love, the short story, the maxim or the novel. A fire of dry grass might equally well have been their publisher. At one point, the thread was lost at the sight of the torture victim's blood, any importance they possessed destroyed. They were written under strain, in anger, fear, rivalry, disgust, cunning, furtive reflection, the illusion of a future, friendship, love. They are intimately bound up with events, that is. I would then glance over them from time to time but seldom read them through.

The notebook might have belonged to no one at all, so remote is the meaning of a man's existence from his journeyings in life, and so hard to tell apart from a mimicry at times quite staggering. Tendencies of this kind were combatted just the same.

The following notes mark the resistance put up by a humanism conscious of its obligations but reluctant to proclaim its virtues, a humanism eager that the inaccessible field be kept free for its suns' imaginings and determined to pay the price for that.

1

As far as possible, teach them to be workman-like—to stick to the goal and not beyond. Beyond is smoke. And where you have smoke, you have change.

2

Don't get bogged down in results.

3

Have the real culminate in action, like a flower tucked into the acrid mouth of a young child. Inexpressible knowledge of the hopeless diamond (life).

4

To be stoical is to be in a rut, with the beautiful eyes of Narcissus. We have taken stock, over every inch of our bodies, of the pain the torturer may one day exact; then, with a heavy heart, have gone out to face him.

5

We belong to no one unless to the gold point of
that lamp, unknown to us and out of reach, which
keeps courage and silence on their guard.

6

The poet strives to turn *old enemies* into *loyal foes*,
for any fruitful future will depend on how well he
has planned ahead—especially when so many sails
are rising, twining, sinking and being decimated
in which the wind from the mainland surrenders
its heart to the wind from the abyss.

7

This war will drag on beyond any platonic armis-
tice. Political concepts will go on being sown
after a show of argument on both sides, amid
the upheavals and under cover of a hypocrisy sure
of its rights. Don't smile. Put aside scepticism and
resignation and prepare your mortal soul to
confront, within these walls, demons that have the
cold-blooded genius of microbes.

8

The moment the instinct for survival gives way
to the instinct for possession, reasonable human
beings lose all sense of their probable lifespan and
day-to-day equilibrium. They grow hostile to

small chills in the atmosphere and submit without further ado to whatever evil and deceit might require of them. Under a maleficent hailstorm their miserable existence simply crumbles away.

9

After fumbling about a bit at the beginning, Mad Arthur has now given himself over, with all the decisiveness of his strong-willed nature, to our hazardous games of chance. His hunger for action must make do with carrying out the precise task I assign to him. He does as I ask and contains himself for fear of getting a good scolding! God knows what hornet's nest his fearlessness would land him in otherwise. Faithful Arthur, like a soldier of old!

10

No amount of authority, no amount of planning and ingenuity can replace a scrap of conviction in the pursuit of truth. A commonplace I think I have improved.

11

My brother, the Tree Surgeon, whom I'm still without news of, used to joke about being on intimate terms with the cats of Pompeii. By the time we found out that this generous creature had been deported, his prison had closed behind him; chains defied his courage; Austria held him.

12

What brought me into the world and will usher me out of it only interferes at moments when I am too feeble to resist. An old lady when I was born, an unknown young woman when I die.

One and the same passer-by.

13

Time seen through an image is time that has faded from view. Being and time are quite different. An image when it has transcended being and time shimmers with eternity.

14

Having twice put him conclusively to the test, I have no trouble convincing myself that the thief who has somehow slipped into our midst is beyond redemption. A pimp (he even boasts about it), spiteful in the extreme, going to pieces before the enemy, wallowing in the horrors he reports, like a pig in offal—nothing to look forward to, other than the most serious troubles, from this runaway slave. Likely, moreover, to introduce a vile fluid here.

I will do the thing myself.

15

The children get bored on Sundays. Sparrow suggests a twenty-four-day week that would cut out Sundays. In other words, adding one hour from Sunday to each of the twenty-four days, preferably the hour spent at table, since there's no more dry bread.

But let there be no more talk of Sundays!

16

Intelligence with the angel, our prime concern.

(Angel: that which, in man, keeps the word of the utmost silence, the meaning that cannot be pinned down, free from any compromise with religion. A tuner of lungs, gilding the vitamin-rich vines of the impossible. Knows the blood, disregards the celestial. Angel: a candle leaning north of the heart.)

17

I'm always glad at heart to stop off at Forcalquier, share a meal with the Bardouins, shake hands with Marius the printer and Figuière. These good people are friendship's citadel on the hill. Whatever hinders clear thinking and slows up trust has been banished from here. We have been wedded, once and for all, in the presence of the essential.

18

Keep the imaginary part for later; it, too, is susceptible of action.

19

The poet cannot remain for long in the stratosphere of the Word. He must curl up in fresh tears and push on into his own estate.

20

I think of that army of deserters, hungry for dictatorship, whom those who survive the Faustian algebra of these times will perhaps see back in power in this mindless country.

21

Bitter future, bitter future, a round dance in a briar of roses . . .

22

TO THE PRUDENT: It's snowing on the Maquis and the hunt for us is always on. You whose house does not weep, whose avarice has crushed out love, the fire that warms you, day after day, is a sicknurse. Too late. The cancer in you has spoken. Our native country has been stripped of its powers.

23

The present, an embattled parapet . . .

24

France has the reactions of a piece of human flot-
sam disturbed during its siesta. Let us hope that the
caulkers and shipwrights busy in the Allied camp
do not prove wreckers in their turn . . .

25

Noon separated from day. Midnight cut off from
men. Midnight with its putrid knell that one
o'clock, two o'clock, three o'clock, four o'clock
cannot muzzle.

26

Time can no longer look to the clock for support;
today, the hands claw at one another on the clock
face of man. Time is dog grass and man will
become the grass's sperm.

27

Léon maintains that mad dogs are beautiful. I
believe him.

28

There's a species of man who is always one step
ahead of his own excrement.

29

This age of ours, with its peculiar way of nurturing things, hastens the prosperity of scum, who step gaily over the barriers that society once put up against them. Will the same mechanism that now acts as a stimulus to them, on breaking, break them too, once its hideous resources have been exhausted?

(And as few survivors as possible from that particular malady!)

30

Archduke confides to me that it was on joining the Resistance that he found himself. Prior to that, he had been a froward and mistrustful actor in his life. Insincerity was poisoning him. Little by little, he was being overcome by a barren sadness. Today, he *loves*, spends out, commits himself, goes naked, provokes. I think very highly of this alchemist.

31

I keep my writings short. I can hardly be *away* for long. To write at length would turn into an obsession. The adoration of the shepherds is no longer of any use to the planet.

32

A man without faults is a mountain without crevasses. He's of no interest to me.

(A rule for water-diviners and worriers.)

33

Redbreast, my friend, arriving this autumn when the gardens were deserted, a landslide of memories has been brought down by your song that the ogres would love to hear about.

34

Wed, and do not wed, your home.

35

You will be part of the fruit's savour.

36

A time when an exhausted sky sinks deep into the earth and man in his death agony is scorned on both sides.

37

Revolution and counter-revolution are donning their masks, preparing for combat once again.

Short-lived candour! After the combat of eagles comes the combat of octopuses. The genius of man, who thinks he has discovered all-encompassing truths, turns truths which kill into truths which *authorize* one to kill. The show put on by these backward-looking visionaries, fighting at the front of an armour-plated and exhausted universe! While the collective neuroses grow ever more pronounced in the eye of myth and symbol, psychic man tortures life, without, it seems, feeling the slightest remorse. The hideous flower, the *outlined* flower, revolves its black petals in the mad flesh of the sun. Where is the source? Where the remedy? When will the economy finally change its ways?

38

They go down under the sheer weight of their prejudices or drunk with enthusiasm for their bogus principles. Have them work together and exorcize their demons; lighten their tread, make them supple and sinewy; then convince them that, beyond a certain point, the importance of received ideas is altogether relative and that the 'matter in hand' is, in any case, a matter of life or death, not of some nuance one would like to see recognized by a civilization that may well sink without trace on the ocean of destiny—these are the things for which I struggle to win the approval of those around me.

39

We are torn between hunger for knowledge and despair at having known. The goad won't abandon its sting, nor we our hope.

40

Discipline, you're bleeding all over!

41

Were it not sealed tight with tedium at times, the heart would stop beating.

42

Between the two rifle shots that would decide his fate, he had time to call a fly 'Madame'.

43

Mouth, which used to decide if this was mourning or marriage, poison or potion, sickness or beauty— what has become of bitterness and tenderness, its dawn?

Hideous head, grown irritable and corrupt!

44

Friends, snow is awaiting snow, for a task to perform, simple and pure, at the boundary of earth and air.

45

I dream of a benevolent country garlanded with flowers, irritated suddenly by the deliberations of its elders but moved at the same time by the zealousness of certain gods in their dealings with women.

46

An act is virgin, even when repeated.

47

Martin, who comes from Reillanne, calls us the *catimini*, the 'secret ones'.

48

I'm not frightened, merely giddy. I must break down the distance between the enemy and myself. Confront him *horizontally*.

49

What might seem enticing about oblivion is that the most beautiful day there can be any day at all.

(Cut down this branch. No swarm will ever hang from it.)

50

Over and against whatever's out there, against ALL THAT: a Colt 45 with its promise of sunrise!

51

Uproot them from their native earth. Set them down in what you presume to be the harmonious soil of the future, bearing in mind that success can only ever be partial. Have them progress through the senses. That is the secret of my 'skill'.

52

'The anvil's mice'. The image would have appealed to me in the past. It suggests a swarm of sparks decimated in its own lightning flash. (The anvil is cold, the iron not red-hot, the imagination aghast.)

53

Having the mistral blowing didn't help matters. With every hour that passed, my fears increased, with little reassurance to be had from the presence of Cabot watching the road for passing convoys that might stop to launch an attack. The first container exploded as it struck the ground. Driven on by the wind, the fire spread to the woods and had soon made a blot on the horizon. The plane altered course slightly and came in for a second run. The cylinders swinging from their multicoloured silks got scattered over an enormous area. We battled for hours in an infernal glare, splitting up into three groups: one lot fighting the fire, doing what they could with axes and spades; a second lot gone off in search of stray arms and explosives and bringing them to the waiting truck; a third providing us with cover. From the tops of pines, panicking squirrels leapt like tiny comets into the blaze.

As for the enemy, we just managed to avoid him. Dawn crept up on us before he did.

(Beware of anecdotes. They're railway stations where the stationmaster loathes the signalman!)

54

Starlight in the month of May . . .

Whenever I look up at the sky now, my jaw swims with nausea. I no longer hear the *moan of pleasure*, the murmur of a woman half open, welling up from the freshness within. Ash from a prehistoric cactus is blowing my desert apart! I'm no longer *capable* of dying . . .

Cyclone, cyclone, cyclone . . .

55

Never definitively formed, man is the keeper of his contrary. The orbits his cycles describe vary according to the forces to which he is, or is not, subject. As for the mysterious depressions and absurd inspirations that rise up from the great crematorium outside, how hard it is to ignore them. Ah! to move generously along the seasons of the almond shell, while the almond within beats free . . .

56

A poem is all furious ascension; poetry, the play of arid riverbanks.

57

The source is rock, the tongue severed.

58

Word, storm, ice and blood will eventually come together in one great frost.

59

If man did not close his eyes *out of majesty* from time to time, he would eventually see nothing worth looking at.

60

Light up the imagination of those who stammer when they mean to speak, who blush when they state their view. They are staunch partisans.

An officer over from North Africa is surprised that my 'bloody Maquisards', as he calls them, speak a language he cannot understand, his ear being hostile to 'speaking in images'. I point out to him that slang is merely picturesque, whereas the language we are accustomed to using here has its source in the wonder communicated by the creatures and things we live in intimate daily contact with.

62

No will testifies to our inheritance.

63

You only fight well for a cause which you yourself have shaped and which you then get burnt identifying with.

64

'What will they do with us, *afterwards*?' This is the question that bothers Minot, who, at the ripe old age of seventeen, adds, 'As for myself, perhaps I'll revert back to the good-for-nothing I was at fifteen . . .' This child, who relies far too much on the example of his comrades, whose goodwill is all too impersonally of a piece with theirs, never takes stock of his own resources. Right now this is a blessing. I rather fear that *afterwards* he will take up once again with those charming lizards whose heedlessness is watched eagerly by the cats . . .

65

The quality of those in the Resistance is not, alas, everywhere the same. For every Joseph Fontaine, who has the rectitude and tenor of a ploughman's furrow, for every François Cuzin, Claude Dechavannes, André Grillet, Marius Bardouin, Gabriel Besson, Doctor Jean Roux or Roger Chaudon converting the granary at Oraison into a castle perilous, how many elusive charlatans there are, more concerned with enjoying themselves than with producing. You can be sure that, come the liberation, these cocks of oblivion will be crowing loudly in our ears . . .

66

The moment I yield to that foreboding which dictates man's cowardice in life, I bring into the world a host of undying friendships that comes rushing to my aid.

67

Armand, the weatherman, calls his job 'the Department of Enigmas'.

68

Dregs in the brain: east of the Rhine. Moral chaos: this side of the river.

69

I see mankind ruined by political perversion, confusing action and atonement, and naming conquest his own annihilation.

70

The devils' alcohol quietly doing its work.

71

Night, swift as the boomerang we have carved from our bones, and whistling, whistling . . .

72

In action, be primitive; in foresight, a strategist.

73

If the grass's subsoil is to be believed, where a pair of crickets were singing last night, prenatal existence must indeed have been heavenly.

74

Alone and manifold. Watching and sleeping like a sword in its scabbard. A stomach in which foods are kept separate. A candle's altitude.

75

Rather depressed by this wavelength (London), just enough to arouse a longing for help.

76

To Carlate, who was going off at a tangent, I said, 'You can busy yourself with the things of death when you are dead. We'll no longer be with you. We need all the strength we can muster to do the job properly and see it through to the end. I won't have our paths weighed down with fog just because clouds are stifling your summits. The time is ripe for metamorphosis. Make the most of it or get out.'

(Carlate's fond of solemn rhetoric. He's a desperate windbag, a fatty infrared.)

77

How can you hide from what is *meant* to be part of you? (The mistake made by modernity.)

78

What matters most in certain situations is mastering one's euphoria in time.

79

I thank whatever lucky star has allowed us to have the poachers of Provence fighting on our side. The knowledge these primitives have of the forest, their gift for calculation and their keen flair, no matter what the weather—I would be surprised if a failing were to come about from that quarter. I shall see to it that they are given shoes fit for gods!

80

Our star-sickness is incurable, yet life fiendishly gives us the illusion of health. Why? In order to squander life and poke fun at health?

(I must resist my inclination for vapid pessimism of this kind, an intellectual heritage . . .)

81

Acquiescence lights up the face. Refusal gives it beauty.

82

The almond and the olive tree, one sober, the other dreamy and cantankerous—on the open fan of twilight, may our curious health stand guard.

83

The poet, guardian of life's infinite faces.

84

You lay bare a person's soul when you go back on your intimacy with them, while at the same time taking responsibility for their development. Bound hand and foot, I suffer that fate against my will and ask that person to forgive me.

85

Icy curiosity. Objectless appraisal.

86

The purest harvests are sown in a soil that doesn't exist. They rule out gratitude, their only debt being to spring.

87

LS, thank you for ManDrop Durance 12. It goes into operation from tonight. Make sure the young team assigned to the field doesn't slip into the habit of appearing too often on the streets of Durance-ville. Girls and cafes dangerous for more than a minute. But don't pull too tightly on the reins, I don't want a squealer in the team. No communication outside the network. Stamp out bragging. Check all intelligence against two sources. Allow for fifty per cent fancy in most cases. Teach your men to be attentive, to give an exact report, to set down the arithmetic of a given situation. Bring together rumours and sum up. Drop point and letterbox with the Friend of the Wheat. Waffen operation possible, foreigners' camp at Les Mées, with overflow onto Jews and Resistance. Spanish republicans in real danger. Urgent you warn them. For yourself, avoid combat. ManDrop sacred. In the event of an alert, disperse. Other than to rescue captured comrade, never let the enemy know you exist. Intercept suspects. I leave it to you to judge. The camp will never be revealed. The camp doesn't exist, only charcoal kilns that don't give off smoke. No washing hung out when the planes come over, and all men under trees or in the scrub. No one will come to see you on my behalf, apart from the Friend of the Wheat and the Swimmer. With the men in your team, be strict and considerate. Friendship muffles discipline. When working, always do a few kilos more than the others, without taking pride in the fact. Eat and smoke conspicuously less than they do. Don't favour one person over another. Tolerate only spontaneous, gratuitous lies. Don't let them call across to one another. Let them keep their bodies and their bedding clean. Let them learn to sing quietly and not to whistle tunes that stick in the head, to tell the truth exactly as it presents itself. At night, they should keep to the side of the path. Suggest precautions but allow them the merit of finding them out for themselves. Rivalry excellent. Oppose monotonous habits and encourage those you don't want dying out too soon. Last but not least, love the ones they love, at the same moment as they do. Add, don't divide. All well here. Affectionately. HYPNOS.

88

How can you hear what I am saying? I'm so far away . . .

89

François, worn out after five straight nights on alert, says, 'I'd gladly swap my sabre for a cup of coffee!' François is twenty.

90

In the past, names were given to the different portions of time—this was a day, that was a month, this empty church a year. Any second now, we will be face to face with death at its most violent and life at its most clearly defined.

91

We roam in the vicinity of wells that have been sealed off from their waters.

92

All that has the face of anger and does not raise its voice.

93

The struggle to endure.

The symphony that buoyed us up has fallen silent. We must trust in the alternation of powers. So many mysteries have been neither fathomed nor destroyed.

94

I was examining a tiny snake sliding between two stones this morning, when Félix cried out, 'The slow-worm of grief.' The loss of Lefèvre, killed last week, flares up with all the force of superstition in an image.

95

The darkness of the Word leaves me sluggish and immune. I take no part in the dreamlike agony. Dispassionate as stone, I am the mother of distant cradles.

96

You can't reread what you have written but you can sign your name.

97

The plane flies low. The invisible pilots jettison their night garden, then activate a brief light tucked in under the wing of the plane to notify us that it's over. All that remains is to gather up the scattered treasure. So it is with the poet ...

98

The flightpath of a poem. Its presence should be *felt* by all.

99

He reminded me of a dead partridge, the poor invalid, who, after being stripped of the few rags he possessed, was murdered by the militia at Vachères, who accused him of harbouring 'partisans'. Before finishing him off, the gangsters enjoyed themselves at great length with a girl who was part of the expedition. With one eye torn out and his chest stoved in, the innocent man took in this hell AND THEIR LAUGHTER.

(We have captured the girl.)

100

We must overcome our rage and disgust and see that they are shared by others; our influence will gain in quality and scope, as will our morale.

101

Imagination, my child.

102

Memory has no control over what we remember. And what we remember is helpless in the face of memory. Happiness no longer *surfaces*.

103

A yard of entrails to measure the odds.

104

Our eyes alone can still cry out.

105

To and fro goes the spirit, like that insect which, the moment the lamp is out, scrapes at the kitchen, upsetting the silence, poking about in the dirt.

106

Harrowing obligations.

107

You can't make a bed for tears as you would for a passing visitor.

108

Impassioned powers and strict rules of action.

109

These flowers with their fragrant mass, to brighten the night now falling on our tears.

110

Eternity is not much longer than life.

111

Light has been banished from our eyes. It's buried somewhere in our bones. It's our turn now to hunt for it and put back its crown.

112

The prelapsarian seal of cosmic approval.

(In the narrows of my night, may this grace be granted me, more overwhelming, more significant even, than those signs seen from so great a height that there's no need to imagine them.)

113

Be on intimate terms with what will come to pass, not in a religion (a senseless solitude), only in that succession of dead ends where, with nothing to nourish it, the face of your loved one tends to fade from view.

114

I will write no poem of consent.

115

In the Garden of Gethsemane, who was the odd man out?

116

Don't take undue account of the duplicity you meet with in people. In reality, the seam is sectioned at numerous points. Let this be a stimulus rather than a source of irritation.

117

Claude tells me, 'Women are queens of the absurd. The more a man commits himself, the more they complicate that commitment. Ever since the day I became a "partisan", I haven't once felt unhappy or disappointed . . .'

There will be plenty of time to teach Claude that nobody carves out of his own life without cutting himself.

118

Woman of punishment.

Woman of resurrection.

119

I think of the woman I love. All of a sudden, her face is veiled. Even the void is ill today.

120

You hold a match to the lamp, yet no light is shed by the flame you've lit. Only a long way off does the circle shine.

121

I aimed at the lieutenant, Bloodspat at the colonel. The flowering gorse concealed us behind its flamboyant yellow vapour. Jean and Robert threw the grenades. The little enemy column immediately beat a retreat. Except for the machine-gunner, but he didn't have time to become dangerous; his belly exploded. We used the two cars to make our getaway. The colonel's briefcase was full of interest.

122

Fontaine-la-Pauvre, the prodigal fountain.

(The march has left us with our hips sawn through and our mouths hollowed out.)

123

A moving appetite for conscience in these young men. None of the endless upstairs-downstairs of their fathers. Oh! to be able to set them on the right path where the human condition is concerned, for you can rest assured that, sooner or later, it will need rehabilitating. Yet, since God takes no part in our quarrels and the stranglehold of origins senses that it is loosing its grip, the new experts will need an intellectual scope and a grasp of detail of which I have yet to see any sign.

124

CAVE-FRANCE.

125

Let the mind find its own way about without the aid of staff maps.

126

Between reality and the account you give of it, there is your own life, which magnifies reality, and this Nazi abjection, which ruins that account.

127

There will come a time when the nations playing hopscotch on the universe will be as close-knit as the organs of the body and one in their economy.

What will become then of that narrow stream in man, his daydreams and his flights of fancy? Bursting with machines, will the brain still be able to safeguard its existence? Like a sleepwalker, man advances towards the murderous minefields, led on by the song of the inventors . . .

128

The baker hadn't even had time to unhook the iron shutters of his shop before the village was under siege, gagged, hypnotized, unable to make the slightest move. Two companies of SS and a detachment of militia had it pinned down under the muzzle of their machine-guns and mortars. Then the ordeal began.

The inhabitants were thrown out of their houses and ordered to assemble on the main square. Keys to be left in their doors. An old man, hard of hearing, who did not respond quickly enough to the order, saw the four walls and roof of his barn blown to bits by a bomb. I had been up since four. Marcelle had come up to my shutters and whispered the alarm. I had realized at once that it would be pointless trying to break through the cordon surrounding the village and get out to the countryside. I quickly changed lodgings. The empty house where I took refuge would allow me, if the worst came to the worst, to put up an effective armed resistance. I could follow from behind the yellowed curtains of the window the nervous comings and goings of the occupying forces. Not one of my men was present in the village. I took comfort in the thought. A few miles from there, they would be following my instructions and lying low. I could hear blows being delivered, punctuated by cursing. The SS had caught a young mason on his way home after emptying his traps. His fright marked him out for their tortures. A voice leant, screaming, over the swollen body: 'Where is he? Take us to him,' followed by silence. A shower of kicks and rifle butts. An insane rage took hold of me, dispelling my anguish. Sweat poured from my hands as I clenched my revolver, rejoicing in its pent-up powers. I calculated that the poor creature would remain silent for five minutes more, then inevitably would *speak*. I felt ashamed wanting him to die before the time was up. Then, issuing from every street, came a flood of women, children and old men, making their way to the assembly point according to an *organized plan*. Taking their time, they hurried forward, literally streaming over the SS and paralysing them 'in all sincerity'. The mason was left for dead. Furious, the patrol pushed its way through the crowd and marched off. With infinite prudence now, anxious, kind eyes glanced in my direction, passing like beams of light over my window. I partially revealed myself and my pale face broke into a smile. I was bound to these people by a thousand threads of trust, not one of which was to break.

I loved my fellow creatures fiercely that day, far beyond the call of sacrifice.

129

We are like those frogs who, in the austerity of the marshes at night, call to but cannot see one another, bending the fatal arc of the universe to their cry of love.

130

From the debris of mountains, I have put together men who, for a time at least, will embalm the glaciers.

131

At every meal taken together, we invite liberty to sit down. The seat remains empty but the place is laid.

132

It seems that the imagination which in varying degrees haunts the mind of every living creature is quick to abandon it when the latter has only the 'impossible' and the 'inaccessible' as ultimate mission to propose. Poetry, it has to be allowed, is not everywhere sovereign.

133

'Charitable work must be kept up, for man is not naturally charitable.' Rubbish. Oh, what murderous drivel!

134

We are like those fish trapped alive in the ice on a mountain lake. Matter and nature seem to be protecting them, yet barely limit the fisherman's odds.

135

You don't need to love your fellow men to be of real help to them. All you need is to wish to improve that look in their eyes when they behold someone even more impoverished than themselves, to prolong for a second some agreeable moment in their lives. Once you've adopted this approach, treating each root in turn, their breathing becomes more peaceful. Above all, don't cut out the more arduous paths altogether, for after the effort comes the tearful and fruitful evidence of truth.

136

Youth holds the spade. Let no one snatch it away!

137

The goats are to the right of the flock. (It's good to have cunning and innocence walk side by side when the shepherd is good and the dog steady.)

138

Horrible day! I witnessed, some hundred yards away, the execution of B. I had only to squeeze the trigger of my machine-gun and he could have been saved! We were on the high ground over-looking Céreste, the bushes bursting with wea-pons and at least equal in number to the SS. They didn't know we were there. To the eyes all around me, begging me for the signal to open fire, I replied with a shake of the head ... The June sun sent a polar chill through my bones.

He seemed unaware of his executioners as he fell, and so light that the slightest breath of wind would have lifted him from the ground.

I didn't give the signal because the village had *at all costs* to be spared. What is a village? A village like any other? Perhaps *he* knew, at that final instant?

139

Enthusiasm takes the weight of the years on its shoulders. It's fraudulence that speaks of the century's fatigue.

140

Life began with an explosion and will end with a pact? It's absurd.

141

The counter-terror is this valley filling little by little with mist; these leaves rustling briefly underfoot like fireworks sputtering out; this nicely balanced load; these muffled movements of animals and insects drawing a thousand lines through the tender bark of night; this clover seed on the dimple of the face you kiss; this fire on the moon that will never be a fire; this tiny future whose plans are unknown to us; this brightly coloured bust that folds away with a smile; and this shadow thrown, a few steps further on, by a man who is briefly your companion and crouches there, thinking the leather of his belt is about to give . . . Who cares, then, what time or place the devil has fixed for the rendezvous?

142

A time of raging mountains and fantastic friendship.

143

MOUNTAIN-EVE: That young lady whose seam-less life was exactly the same size as the heart of our night.

144

How moth-eaten your old butterfly bones have become!

145

That happiness which is nothing but anxiety deferred. A blue-tinted happiness, wonderfully unruly, taking pleasure as its springboard, annihilating the present and all its jurisdictions.

146

Roger was delighted at having become in the eyes of his young wife the husband-who-was-hiding-God.

Today, I passed the field of sunflowers the sight of which so inspired him. The heads of these wonderful, insipid flowers were weighed down with drought. It was a few yards from there that his blood was spilt, at the foot of an ancient mulberry tree as deaf to the world as its bark is thick.

147

Will we later be like those craters no longer visited by volcanoes, where the grass yellows on its stem?

148

'Here he comes!' It's two in the morning. The plane has seen our signals and reduced altitude. The breeze won't be a problem for the visitor we're expecting, who's coming in by parachute. The moon is the colour of sage and polished tin. 'A school for poets of the eardrum,' whispers Léon, who always has the right word for the occasion.

149

My arm is in plaster and causing me some pain. Dear Doctor Tall Fellow has made a marvellous job of it, despite the swelling. Luck that my sub-conscious guided my fall in quite the way it did. Otherwise, the grenade I was holding, with its pin out, stood a very good chance of exploding. Luck that the Feldgendarmes heard nothing (they had left the engine of their truck running). Luck that I didn't pass out with my head cracked like a flower pot . . . My comrades congratulate me on my presence of mind. I have difficulty persuading them that no credit is due me. It all went on outside me. After a thirty-foot fall, I felt like a basket of dislocated bones. Fortunately, there was almost nothing of the kind.

150

It's a strange feeling, deciding the fate of certain individuals. Had you not intervened, the dumb waiter of life would have continued on its mediocre round. Whereas here they are delivered up to the most poignant juncture of all . . .

151

Reply 'missing' yourself or you risk being misunderstood.

152

The silence of morning. The apprehension of colour. The *luck* of the sparrowhawk.

153

I see more clearly now the need to simplify, to have everything working together as one, when it comes to deciding whether such and such a thing needs to be done. Man is sorry to have to leave his labyrinth. The age-old myths urge him not to go.

154

The poet, inclined to exaggerate, thinks clearly under duress.

I love these people so enamoured of what their
hearts imagine to be freedom that they offer up
their lives to prevent what little freedom remains
from dying. The virtue of the common man is
marvellous. (Free will, they say, does not exist.
Human beings are defined by cells, by hereditary
traits, by the brief or more extended duration of
their fate . . . Yet between *all that* and mankind is
an enclave of unforeseeables and metamorphoses,
which we must guard the entrance to and make
sure is preserved.)

Amass, then share out. In the mirror of the uni-
verse, be the densest, the most useful and the least
conspicuous part.

We're racked with grief on learning that Robert
G. (Émile Cavagni) is dead, killed in an ambush
at Forcalquier last Sunday. The Germans have
robbed me of my finest brother-in-arms, one
whose helping hand sufficed to ward off a catas-
trophe, whose timely presence had a decisive
influence on the shortcomings that threaten us
all. A man with no formal education but grown
strong in adversity, his kindness never wavered

and his diagnosis was faultless. His conduct was an informed mixture of rousing boldness and good sense. Resourceful, he would carry his advantages through to their utmost conclusion. At forty-five, he walked tall, like a tree of liberty. My love for him was uneffusive and unencumbered. Steadfast.

158

Adjustable wings and smiles free of rancour are what we now find in ourselves when we ponder the vulgar convict camp of thieves and assassins. The man-with-a-fist-like-cancer, the great Murderer within, has moved in our favour.

159

So close is the affinity between the cuckoo and the furtive creatures we have become that whenever that bird—which you hardly ever see, and, even when you do catch sight of one, is always dressed in anonymous grey—lets out its heart-rending song, a long shudder goes through us in response.

160

Dew of humanity, drawing up and concealing its frontiers between first light and the emergence of the sun, between the eyes that open and the heart that remembers.

161

Fulfil with regard to others what you have promised to yourself alone. That is your contract.

162

Now is the time when the poet feels rising in him the noontide powers of ascension.

163

Sing your irridescent thirst.

164

Loyal and vulnerable in the extreme, we counter the gratuitous (another word I have cleansed from my body) with an awareness of events.

165

The fruit is blind. It is the tree that sees.

166

For a heritage to be truly great, the hand of the deceased must be invisible.

167

Ketty the dog takes as much pleasure as we do in gathering the parachute drops. She goes briskly from one to the other without barking, knowing exactly what is required. Once the work is over, she stretches out, happy, on the dune formed by the parachutes and falls asleep.

168

Resistance is nothing but hope. Like the moon of Hypnos, full tonight in all four quarters, tomorrow a view onto the poems coming through.

169

Clarity of vision is the closest wound to the sun.

170

The rare moments of liberty are those when the unconscious becomes conscious and consciousness the void (or mad orchard).

171

The ashes of winter are in the fire that sings of refusal.

172

I pity the man who gets others to pay his debts for him, then compounds those debts with an aura of apparent mindlessness.

173

Some women are like the waves of the sea. Surging forward with all the energy of youth, they break over a rock too high for their return. Henceforth, they are stranded there—stagnant pools, beautiful for a second under lightning, on account of the salt crystals they contain, which little by little become their lives.

174

The loss of truth, the deadweight of that organized ignominy called 'good' (evil, when not depraved but whimsical and inspired, is useful) has opened a wound in man's side that only the hope of the unformulated far horizon (a plenitude of life despaired of) makes bearable. If the absurd is to be lord and master here on earth, then I opt for the absurd, the anti-static, whatever weights the passions in my favour. I'm a man of the riverbanks—of erosion and inflammation—for I cannot always be of the mountain stream.

175

The meadow folk enchant me. I never tire of naming over to myself their frail, good-natured beauty. The field mouse and the mole, brooding children lost in a dream of grass; the slow-worm, son of glass; the cricket, utterly lamb-like; the grasshopper, who clacks and counts her linen; the butterfly, who feigns drunkenness, annoying the flowers with his silent hiccups; the ants, made wise by the boundless green expanse; and, immediately overhead, the meteoric swallows . . .

Meadow—the jewellery box in which the day's treasures are laid.

176

Ever since that kiss in the mountains, time has been governed by the golden summer of her hands and the sidelong ivy.

177

Children perform the delightful miracle of remaining children while seeing the world through our eyes.

178

The colour reproduction of *The Prisoner* by Georges de la Tour, which I have pinned to the whitewashed wall of the room where I work, seems, with time, to reflect its meaning back on our predicament. It makes your heart bleed, yet how refreshing it is! For two years now, not one *réfractaire* has stepped through that door without his eyes smarting at the evidence of that candle. The woman explains, the prisoner listens. The words falling from this red angel's earthly silhouette are life-giving words, words which are immediately of help. In the depths of the dungeon, the minutes of tallow light pull at the features of the seated man, diluting them. Thin as a dry nettle, no memory I can see could quicken his withered flesh. The bowl is a ruin. But the billowing robe suddenly fills the entire dungeon. The power of woman's Word to give birth to the unforeseeable is greater than any dawn.

My gratitude to Georges de la Tour for mastering the Hitlerian darkness with a dialogue between human beings.

179

Come to us who are reeling from sunstroke, O scornless sister, Night!

180

It's the hour when windows slip from their homes and light up at the end of the world where our own world will one day dawn.

181

I envy the child who stoops over the sun's hand-writing, then rushes off to school, brushing aside with a poppy the lines set as punishment *and* the rewards.

182

A lyre for interned mountains.

183

We fight on the bridge thrown between the vulnerable individual and his ricochet at the fountainhead of formal power.

184

Heal the bread. Bring the wine to table.

185

At times I take refuge in the silence of Saint-Just at the Convention of the Ninth Thermidor. I understand—ah! only too well—the *procedure* involved, the crystal shutters closed for ever on *communication*.

186

Are we doomed to be only the beginnings of truth?

187

Action, which has meaning for the living, only has value for the dead, is only complete in the minds of those who inherit and question it.

188

Between the world of reality and myself, there is none of that dreary impenetrability any more.

189

So many people confuse their own ill humour with the spirit of revolt, see a lineage in a surge of feeling. Yet the moment truth finds an enemy worthy of itself, it puts off the armour of ubiquitousness and fights with the resources that are the very essence of its condition. It's impossible to express, this sense of something deep down which, the moment it materializes, vanishes into thin air.

190

How inexorably strange! From this ill-guarded life, somehow to have thrown the quick dice of happiness . . .

191

The rightest hour is when the almond bursts from its restive shell and gives new shape to your solitude.

192

I see hope, the stream in which tomorrow's waters will run, drying up in the gestures of those all around me. The faces I love are wasting away in the nets of expectation, which eats into them like acid. How little help we receive, what scant encouragement! The sea and its shores are the obvious way forward but have been sealed off by the enemy. They are at the back of everyone's mind, the mould for a substance comprised, in equal measure, of the rumour of despair and the certainty of resurrection.

193

So unreceptive has our sleep become that even the briefest of dreams cannot come galloping through to refresh it. The prospect of dying is submerged beneath an inundation of the absolute so all-engulfing that the mere thought of it is enough to lose any desire for the life we cry out for and implore. Once again, we must love one another well, must breathe more deeply than the executioner's lungs.

194

I do violence to myself to ensure that, whatever my mood, my voice remains dipped in ink. It's with a pen like a battering ram, therefore, forever doused, forever relit, serried, tense and in a single breath, that one thing gets written down, another forgotten. Vanity's clockwork doll? I honestly think not. A need to check the evidence, to breathe life into it.

195

If I survive, I know that I shall have to do away with the aroma of these vital years, quietly put my treasure behind me (not bury it away inside) and learn to conduct my life in the simplest manner possible, as in the days when I was searching for, but not yet master of, myself—with naked dissatisfaction, only a glimmer of knowledge and a questioning humility.

196

This man around whom my sympathy is sure to revolve for a while *counts* because his eagerness to serve coincides with a whole halo of auspicious circumstances and with the plans I have for him. Let us work together while there is still time, before whatever it is that brings us together turns unaccountably to hostility.

197

Be of the leap, not of the feast, its epilogue.

198

If only life could be disappointed sleep ...

199

There are two ages for the poet—the age when poetry, in every respect, treats him badly and the age when she allows herself to be furiously kissed. But neither age is clearly defined. And the second is by no means sovereign.

200

It's when you are drunk with sorrow that all that remains of sorrow is the crystal.

201

The way of hiding shimmers in the heat.

202

The presence of desire, like that of the god, is unaware of the philosopher. The philosopher, in return, chastises.

203

Today, I experienced the minute of absolute power and invulnerability. I was a hive flying off to the springs of altitude with all its honey and bees on board.

204

Truth, mechanical infanta, remain earth and murmur amid the impersonal stars!

205

Doubt is at the origin of all greatness. History, being unjust, prides itself on not mentioning the fact. Doubt in this sense is genius. It should not be likened to the uncertain, which comes about when the powers of sensation are broken up.

206

Every ruse I am forced by circumstances to adopt prolongs my innocence. I am carried in the palm of a gigantic hand. Each line there modifies my conduct. And I stand there like a plant in its soil, though my season is of nowhere.

207

Certain acts of mine find a way through my nature like a train through the countryside—through no will of mine and with the same vanishing art.

208

The man who sees only one fountainhead knows only one storm. It interferes with his luck.

209

My inability to organize my life comes from my being faithful, not just to one person but to all those with whom I feel a genuine sense of kinship.

This constancy persists amid clashes and differences of opinion. There's a funny side to it all, for whenever feeling and literal meaning break down in this way, I imagine that the people in question are plotting to do away with me.

210

Your boldness, a wart. Your action, a specious image tainted by self-interest.

(I can still recall the fatuous remark made by that charcoal-burner from Saumanes who claimed that the French Revolution had purged the region of an altogether criminal gentleman, a certain Sade. One of his exploits had consisted in slitting the throats of his farm manager's three daughters. The Marquis's breeches were bulging even before the first beauty had expired . . .

The idiot stuck to his guns, his alpine avarice, needless to say, not wanting to make the slightest concession.)

211

The justicers fade into the distance. Lo! the covetous turn their backs on the airy heather . . .

212

Thrust into the unknown, which burrows deep. Force yourself to keep turning.

213

This morning, I watched Florence making her way back to Mill on the Calavon. The footpath swirled round her—a flowerbed of bickering mice! The chaste back and long legs failed to grow smaller in my eyes. The jujube breasts lingered beneath my teeth. Stirred by each note in turn, I played over her splendid musician's body, unknown to mine, until the foliage, at a turning, stole her from my view.

214

I haven't seen a star light up on the forehead of those about to die, only the pattern cast by a venetian blind which, when raised, afforded a glimpse of an array of objects, heart-rending or resigned, in an enormous room where happy housemaids were milling about.

215

No one quite knows why, yet heads full of slimy sap have turned up in our winter and stuck there ever since. A filthy future is written in their features. Dubois, for example, confirmed and perpetuated by his informer's spartan fat. May the righteous in heaven and a stray bullet grant him the honours of their wit . . .

216

The shepherd cannot possibly be a guide any lon-
ger. So political man, that new farmer general, has
decided.

217

Olivier le Noir asked me for a pan of water to
clean his revolver. I suggested gun grease. But it
was indeed water that was needed. The blood on
the sides of the basin was beyond the range of my
imagination. What point was there picturing the
shameful, broken-down figure, a gun barrel in his
ear, writhing in his own juices? A justicer had
returned, like someone who, after giving the soil
a good turn, wipes the muck from his spade
before looking up with a smile at the burgeoning
young vines.

218

In your conscious body, the reality of the imagi-
nation is a few minutes fast. This gap, which can
never be bridged, forms a gulf that is alien to the
acts of this world. It's never a straightforward dark-
ness, however redolent of warm summer nights,
the religious afterlife, incorruptible childhood.

219

All of a sudden, you remember you have a face. The features which shape that face weren't always racked with grief. Drawn to its varied landscape, creatures gifted with kindness would appear. Nor was it only castaways who succumbed, exhausted, to its spell. The loneliness of lovers could breathe freely there. Look. Your mirror has turned into a fire. Little by little, you remember your age (which had been struck from the calendar), that surplus of existence which, by working at it, you will turn into a bridge. Step back inside the mirror. Arid it may be but at least its fruitfulness has not run dry.

220

I dread not only the anaemia but the feverishness that is sure to set in in the years following the war. Our cosy unanimity, our insatiable hunger for justice, will, I sense, be short-lived, once the bond uniting us in combat has been broken. On the one hand, we prepare to lay claim to an abstraction; on the other, we turn away like blind men from anything likely to alleviate the cruelty of the human condition in our time and allow us to move into the future with a confident step. Already disease is everywhere at war with its remedy. Phantoms rush about giving advice, paying calls—phantoms whose empirical souls are a mare's nest of neuroses and phlegm. This rain now drenching man to the bone is his expectation of aggression, his acquiescence in contempt. We will be quick to forget. We will give up consigning things to the scrapheap, cutting away and healing. We will assume that the dead we have buried have walnuts in their pockets, and that a tree will one day spring up of its own accord.

O Life, if there is still time, give the living a little of your subtle common sense, but without the vanity that would misuse it. And above all, perhaps, convince them that you are not quite as accidental and remorseless as you are said to be. It's not the arrow that is hideous, only the arrowhead.

221

Night Chart

Once more, the new year mingles our eyes.
The tall grass stands watch, its one love the fire
    and the prison at which it gnaws.
Afterwards, the victor's ashes
And a tale of evil;
Afterwards, the ashes of love,
The sweetbriar with its surviving knell;
Afterwards, your ashes,
The imaginary ashes of your life immobile on its
    shadowy cone.

Come, little vixen, lay your head on my knees. I am not happy, and yet you suffice. Night light or meteor, not a swollen heart or future is left on earth. In the twilight marches your murmur can be heard, the den you have lined with mint and rosemary, the whisperings the reds of autumn share with your own light robe. You are the soul of the deep-wombed mountain, its rocks silent behind lips of clay. Let your nostrils quiver. With your hand, close the path behind you and draw the curtain of trees. Little vixen, with the frost and wind, these two stars, for my witness, I place all my fallen hopes in you, for the thistle's victory over rapacious solitude.

223

Life, that cannot and will not trim its sails; life, that the winds leave foundering in mud on the harbour shore, though always ready to rise above torpor; life less and less plenteous, less and less patient— show me my share, should I have one, my just share in the common fate, at the centre of which my singularity stands out yet holds the mixture together.

224

In the past when I went to bed the idea of a temporary death in the arms of sleep was a comfort

to me; today I go to sleep just to live for a few
hours.

225

The child sees the man not in a reliable but in a
simplified light. Therein lies the secret of their
inseparability.

226

A decision that's binding isn't always a source of
strength.

227

Man is capable of doing what he is incapable of
imagining. His mind furrows the galaxy of the
absurd.

228

Who are the martyrs working for? It's in the
commitment of setting sail that greatness lies.
Exemplary lives are made of steam and wind.

229

The colour black houses the *impossible*, alive. Its
mental realm is the seat of the unforeseen, the
paroxystic, in all its forms. Its resplendence is the
poet's escort and girds the man of action.

230

All the virtue of the August sky, all the virtue of our trusted companion, anguish, in the golden voice of the meteor.

231

A few days before his execution, Roger Chaudon said to me, 'On this planet of ours, mankind occasionally has the upper hand but most of the time not. The order in which the ages occur can't be reversed. Ultimately, it's what puts my mind at rest, despite the joy of being alive which shakes me like thunder . . .'

232

The outstanding neither turns the head of its murderer nor moves him to pity. The murderer, alas, has the eyes needed to kill.

233

Bear in mind, without letting it affect you, that the targets evil most enjoys picking off are the unsuspecting ones, the ones it has had plenty of time to approach. All that you have learnt about men—their senseless volte-faces and incurable moodiness, their harlequin-like subjectivity and love of a good brawl—should prompt you, once the action is over, not to linger too long at the scene of your relations.

234

Eyelids, the gates to a happiness as liquid as the flesh of a shellfish; eyelids that the frenzied eye is powerless to capsize; oh, how satisfying are eyelids!

235

Anguish: skeleton and heart; city and forest; dung-hill and magic; incorruptible wilderness; vanquishes only in the mind; victorious; silent; mistress of speech; wife to one and all; and mankind.

236

'My body was vaster than the earth and I knew only a tiny part of it. So manifold are the promises of bliss now stirring in my soul that I beseech you to keep your name known only to ourselves.'

237

In the darkness of our lives, there is not *one* place for Beauty. The whole place is for Beauty.

The Oak Rose

Each of the letters that makes up your name, O Beauty, on the honours roll of human suffering merges with the plane simplicity of the sun, forms part of the giant phrase barring the sky and joins forces with the man bent on outwitting destiny with its indomitable contrary—hope.

Introduction (p. vii) | 'I had the good fortune . . .': Letter from René Char to Gilbert Lely, 17 July 1945 (Jacques Polge collection).

Hypnos | the Greek god of Sleep, son of Nyx (Night) and twin brother of Thanatos (Death). In the *Iliad*, he lulls Zeus to sleep at Hera's request and thereby helps alter the course of the Trojan War in the Greeks' favour. For Char, he is both the deity whose support he and his companions enlist and a symbol of the darkness of Occupied France, in which the body politic is under forcible hypnosis, so to speak, and the country is sleepwalking. In the book's hermetic epigraph, he is shown lulling winter to sleep, then retreating into the counterfeit 'fire' of the full moon (see Fragment 141), under whose auspices Char and his companions go about their work at night, gathering up the arms flown in by Allied parachute drop.

Fragment 3 (p. 3) | mouth of a young child: cf. Psalms 8:2: 'Out of the mouth of babes and sucklings hast thou ordained strength because of thine enemies, that thou mightest still the enemy and the avenger' and Heraclitus' famous image of time (or eternity) as a child playing draughts.

Fragment 9 (p. 7) | Mad Arthur: Bruno Charmasson, known as Arthur. *Arthur-le-fol* has echoes of the *Quest for the Holy Grail*, one of the books Char had by him in the Maquis. Other books that played a part in Char's thinking at this time include Friedrich Hölderlin's *Hyperion* and Blaise Pascal's *Pensées*, a copy of which he took with him when he was flown out to Algiers. He may also have read *The Iliad or the Poem of Force* by Simone Weil (Marseilles: Les Cahiers du Sud, 1940).

Fragment 11 (pp. 7–8) | My brother, the Tree Surgeon: Francis Curel, Char's close childhood friend from l'Isle-sur-Sorgue and a militant communist. Between 15 and 19 September 1943, the Gestapo rounded up 126 suspected Resistance members in the Vaucluse region, 40 of whom were deported. Curel, his wife, brother and mother were among those taken prisoner. Char was present in the town at the time but had been tipped off. Curel was deported to a camp in Linz in Austria, from which he returned in 1945.

Fragment 15 (p. 9) | Sparrow: Passereau in the French. This could be either a nickname or a surname. He has not been identified.

Fragment 17 (p. 9) | Forcalquier: a town perched on a rocky outcrop in the Alpes-de-Haute-Provence. In the French edition, the passage is printed with the following footnote: 'Persons mentioned are referred to by their real names, which were restored in September 1944.'

Marius Testanière: a printer who provided false identity papers for Char and his companions.

Marius Bardouin and Elie Figuière: two among the very first members of Char's group.

Fragment 27 (p. 11) | Léon: Léon Saingermain, alias of Pierre Zyngerman, a Jewish student from Poland who was arrested in Paris and imprisoned for distributing patriotic tracts in 1940 but escaped to England. He was trained by the Bureau Central de Renseignements et d'Action (BCRA), the secret services founded in 1940 by the French government in exile in London, then parachuted into France some time around October 1943 to second Char.

Fragment 30 (p. 12) | Archduke: alias of Camille Rayon who was trained by the BCRA and parachuted into France to coordinate landings and parachute drops in southeast France. In September 1943, he took charge of the Section Atterrissage et Parachutage (SAP) Region 2 (the seven departments covering southeast France), and shortly afterwards appointed Char sector head for the Basses-Alpes.

Fragment 33 (p. 13) | the gardens: the gardens of Les Névons, the large family home in l'Isle-sur-Sorgue, as confirmed by a handwritten note in a copy of the book now in the Bibliothèque Littéraire Jacques Doucet in Paris. What the memories are Char does not say but, in light of the previous fragment, he is probably alluding to the severe beatings he received as a boy from his much older brother, Albert, after the death of their father. Char used to go down to the garden at dawn and box the trunks of trees until he was tough enough to

71

defend himself. Albert, it should also be noted, was a militant Pétainist.

Fragment 37 (pp. 13–14) | the *outlined* flower: the swastika.

Fragment 47 (p. 16) | Martin: member of the Francs-tireurs et Partisans (FTP), established under the Occupation as the military branch of the French Communist Party. His identity is not known. Reillanne is a village a few miles to the north-east of Céreste.

Fragment 53 (pp. 17–18) | Cabot: André Cabot, one of three local gendarmes responsible for diverting vehicles that strayed too close to the fields used for parachute drops. Four drop-zones had been cleared in the countryside around Céreste under Char's command, code-named 'Maréchal', 'Loterie', 'Lux' and 'Touriste'. Char and his companions gathered up fifty-three parachute drops and organized twenty-one secret arms and munitions depots, none of which was discovered.

Fragment 64 (pp. 20–1) | Minot: nickname for the youngest member of Char's group, a boy from Avignon who has not been identified.

Fragment 65 (p. 21) | Joseph Fontaine: joint second-in-command for the Basses-Alpes of the Noyautage des Administrations Publiques (NAP), a movement founded in 1942 with the aim of infiltrating the Vichy government.

François Cuzin: a philosophy teacher at the *lycée* in Dignes.

Claude Dechavannes: nicknamed Tintin, he was the head of the Valensole-Centre sector.

André Grillet: Grillet lived in a village near Forcalquier; he and his wife Ciska belonged to the network run by Maurice Buckmaster, head of the French section of the Special Operations Executive in London.

Marius Bardouin: among the very first members of Char's group.

Gabriel Besson: a close comrade of Char's from Manosque. On the night of 28 February 1946, he was shot in the back while parking his van outside the railway station at Manosque (see note to Fragment 215).

Doctor Jean Roux: a local physician who had a practice in l'Isle-sur-Sorgue and was one of several doctors who served the Resistance.

Roger Chaudon: Chaudon ran an agricultural cooperative in Oraison and was one of Char's closest comrades in the Basses-Alpes. In July 1944, a few days after being flown out to Algiers to help prepare the Allied invasion of southern France, Char learnt that ten or so of his companions, including Chaudon, Cuzin and Louis Martin-Bret, a socialist town councillor from Manosque, had been captured following a meeting of the Comité Départemental de Libération in Oraison by a group of French militia disguised as Resistance members. Transferred to Gestapo headquarters at Marseilles, they were interrogated and tortured before being shot on 18 July in a valley outside Signes, in the Haut Var. Their bodies were among the thirty-nine found in a mass grave there on 17 September 1944; autopsies revealed that a number of them had been buried alive.

Fragment 67 (p. 21) | Armand: alias of Marcel Chaumien.

Fragment 76 (p. 23) | Carlate has not been identified. His nickname recalls the French *écarlate* (scarlet), the colour worn by cardinals of the Roman Catholic church in memory of the blood of Christ and the Christian martyrs.

Fragment 87 (pp. 25–7) | LS: Léon Saingermain (see note to Fragment 27).

ManDrop Durance 12: a ManDrop (*homodépôt*) was a drop-zone that could also be used as a landing strip.

Duranceville: code name for the village Oraison, on the banks of the Asse, a tributary of the Durance.

Friend of the Wheat: Roger Chaudon (see note to Fragment 27).

Les Mées: village in the Alpes-de-Hautes-Provence where the Vichy government had set up a labour camp for 'undesirable aliens'. Among several Jews whose safekeeping Char watched over during the war were his first wife Georgette, née Engelhard, and her parents, and the poet and Marquis de Sade biographer Gilbert Lely.

the Swimmer: Gabriel Besson (see note to Fragment 65). A 'swimmer' was a liaison officer entrusted with a particularly difficult mission.

Fragment 89 (p. 27) | François: probably François Cuzin (see note to Fragment 65).

Fragment 94 (p. 24) | Félix: Félix Bagnini.

Lefèvre: Gustave Lefèvre, former member of the International Brigade and head of the first Maquis in the village of Banon, on the Plateau d'Albion. He was killed by the head of the local militia in an ambush in Manosque on the night of 2–3 September 1943.

Fragment 99 (p. 29) | the poor invalid: Arthur Vincent, goatherd. His brother Norbert was active in the SAP. Before leaving the village, the militia set fire to the farm and threw Vincent, still alive, into the blaze. The village of Vachères was home to several important members of the Resistance, including the *frères* Barthelemy, men's outfitters in Marseilles who provided clothes for Char's comrades and were later denounced to the Gestapo and executed.

Fragment 115 (p. 32) | Garden of Gethsemane: cf. W. H. Auden's remark in 'The Martyr as Dramatic Hero': 'Far from rushing joyfully upon death, in the Garden of Gethsemane, Christ prays in agony that the cup shall pass from him.' (*Secondary Worlds*, London: Faber & Faber, 1968).

Fragment 117 (p. 32) | Claude: probably Claude Dechavannes (see note to Fragment 65).

Fragment 121 (p. 33) | Bloodspat: probably Bruno Charmasson's brother, Jean, a militant communist from l'Isle-sur-Sorgue.

Jean and Robert have not been identified.

Fragment 128 (pp. 35–7) | the incident described here took place on 29 June 1944, a week after the execution of Roger Bernard evoked in Fragment 138.

Marcelle: Marcelle Pons, her mother Marie and her young daughter Mireille looked after Char during this period. Marcelle carried messages throughout the region and is the 'little vixen' of Fragment 222. In the French edition, the passage is printed with this footnote: 'It was chance, surely, that chose me as prince that day, not the heart of the village that had ripened for me? (1945).' In an annotated copy of the book now in the Bibliothèque Littéraire Jacques Doucet in Paris, Char has written alongside this passage: 'I was wrong to write this note.'

Fragment 138 (pp. 39) | B.: Roger Bernard, a young poet and printer from the village of Pertuis in the Lubéron, whom Char kept an anxious, fatherly eye on. One of Bernard's roles was to carry messages from a radio-post in the village of Flaqueyrole to Char in Céreste. Though instructed never to carry a gun on his person, on 22 June 1944, he was stopped and searched by an SS patrol who found a pistol in his rucksack. As is clear from the introduction Char wrote to a collection of Bernard's poems which he edited at the end of the war (*Ma faim noir déjà*, Éditions des Cahiers d'Art, 1945), he and his men were not present at Bernard's execution; the only witness was a local farmer, who told him that Bernard 'stood very straight, very light and obstinately silent'.

Fragment 143 (p. 41) | Mountain-Eve: has not been identified.

Fragment 146 (p. 41) | Roger: Roger Bernard (see note to Fragment 138).

Fragment 149 (p. 42) | Doctor Tall Fellow: Doctor Jean Roux (see note to Fragment 65).

Fragment 157 (p. 40) | Robert G. (Émile Cavagni): a key member of Char's group. On the night of 7–8 June 1944, Cavagni and ten other Resistance members were killed while trying to take Forcalquier from the Germans. Immediately after the Normandy landings on 6 June 1944, General Koenig, Commander of the Forces Françaises de l'Intérieur (FFI), had ordered a general uprising throughout Occupied France. Char and his comrades considered the order foolish and premature and the cause of unnecessary loss of many lives.

Fragment 178 (pp. 49–50) | Georges de la Tour: Char is thought to have discovered the work of Georges de la Tour at a 1934 Paris exhibition of seventeenth-century realist painting. *The Prisoner*, as it was then called, is today known as *Job Mocked by His Wife*. A colour reproduction of the painting was published in the surrealist review *Minotaure* in 1935.

réfractaire: term for young Frenchmen who refused to register for the Service du Travail Obligatoire (STO), a forced labour scheme introduced on 16 February 1943 that required all Frenchmen between the ages of twenty-one and thirty to carry out civilian work in Germany. In exchange, the Nazis allowed a number of French military prisoners of war to return home. Many *réfractaire*s joined the Resistance.

Fragment 185 (p. 47) | Saint-Just: one of the principal architects of the French Constitution of 1793. At the Convention of the Ninth Thermidor, the National Convention voted for the execution of Robespierre, Saint-Just and other revolutionary radicals, prompting the Thermidorian Reaction, a backlash against the atrocities perpetrated during the Reign of Terror.

Fragment 204 (p. 55) | infanta: in Littré's French dictionary, one of the definitions of *infante* is 'a woman of questionable virtue'.

Fragment 210 (pp. 57) | Saumanes: a village in the Vaucluse famous for its fortified castle formerly belonging to the Marquis de Sade's uncle and a few miles from Sade's own château at La Coste. Like the allusion to Saint-Just in Fragment 185, the presence of Sade gives a radical inflexion to the humanism celebrated in the book's foreword. Sade was an important figure for Char, as he was and remains for many writers in France, not least for his critique of the Enlightenment. In the context of the book, their presence is perhaps best understood in the light of the remarks on good and evil in Fragment 174.

Fragment 211 (p. 57) | justicers: though not much used in modern English, this is the term Char employs in contradistinction to 'vigilante'. The word is used a second time, in what is probably the most unsettling passage in the book, in Fragment 217.

Fragment 213 (p. 58) | Florence: Lucienne Bernard, wife of Roger Bernard. After the war, she modelled from time to time for the painter Henri Matisse.

Fragment 215 (p. 58) | Dubois: Georges Dubois, expelled from the SAP by Char for embezzling funds. Rightly or wrongly, Char and his companions believed that Dubois, a correspondant for the communist daily *Rouge-Midi*, was responsible for the murder of Gabriel Besson in 1946, in connection with a vicious smear campaign orchestrated by the paper during the winter of 1945–46. Though fiercely anti-Stalinist, Char was sympathetic to the communists at the time, many of whom had fought at his side in the Resistance. In spring 1946, Dubois was expelled from the French Communist Party.

Fragment 217 (pp. 59) | Olivier le Noir: René Obadia, alias Pioche (pick or mattock), one of two hardened military advisers parachuted into the Groupes Francs from England to train Resistance fighters in close combat and the use of explosives. He also carried out sabotage operations in the region, notably blowing up part of an important aluminium plant at Gardanne.

Fragment 220 (pp. 60–1) | have walnuts in their pockets: 'One day, during the war, I was asked to find an empty strip of land on the plateau de Valensole where Allied planes in difficulty could land. I find a large field that fits the bill but there's a magnificent three-hundred-year-old walnut tree in the middle of it. The owner of the field was willing to rent it to me, but stubbornly refused to cut down the beautiful tree. I eventually told him why we needed the land, whereupon he agreed. We start clearing away the soil around the base of the tree; we follow the taproot.... At the end of the root, we find the bones of a knight

79

buried in his armour. The man must have been a mediaeval knight . . . and he had a walnut in his pocket when he was killed, for the base of the taproot was exactly level with his thigh-bone. The walnut tree had sprouted in the grave.' Quoted in Paul Veyne, *René Char en ses poèmes* (Paris: Gallimard, 1990), pp. 186–7.

Fragment 222 (p. 62) | little vixen: Marcelle Pons, Char's lover during his time in Céreste (see note to Fragment 128). A fox was the emblem adopted by the French Resistance in the Basses-Alpes. 'La Renardière' (fox's den) was also the name of a farm owned by the Roux family that was rented out to local peasants in exchange for food (wheat, eggs and chicken), part of which was used to feed Char's group.

ACKNOWLEDGEMENTS

The present translation was begun many years ago and has been through more revisions than I care to remember. It is in part a labour of love and in part a response to the ungainliness of previous English versions. To elucidate some of the obscurer passages in the French, I have girded myself with dictionaries and ventured into the translation by Paul Celan—but always under the watchful eye of German-speaking friends. I have also adopted Celan's solution for the book's title, a 'literal' translation of which muddies the meaning of *feuillet* and makes a dog's breakfast of English syntax. 'Leaves from the Journal of Hypnos' would be an accurate gloss but is too ponderous to be of use.

Translation is an arduous business and would be an altogether thankless task without the conversation and encouragement of others. For their patience and generosity, I am especially grateful to Lorenza Garcia, Steven Jaron, the late Tina Jolas, Radhika Jones, James Lasdun, Matthew Mars-Jones, John Naughton, Anthony Rudolf, Anne Serre, Mireille Sidoine-Audouy and Ian de Toffoli; for their kindly interest in trying to help the project along, David Brooks, Marie-Claude Char, Geoffrey O'Brien, Michael Schmidt, John A. Scott, Richard Sieburth, George Steiner and Mark Strand; and for his invaluable assistance in ensuring the accuracy of the notes, Antoine Coron, Keeper of Rare Books at the Bibliothèque Nationale de France.

Thanks are also due to my publishers at Seagull Books for agreeing to print the journal as a book in its own right, and to the editors of *Grand Street* and *Harper's*, in which parts of the translation, sometimes in slightly different form, first appeared.

Mark Hutchinson
Paris, 2014